RESTART PIANO

Written by Karen Marshall
Selected arrangements by Heather Hammond

T0056421

&

WISE PUBLICATIONS
part of The Music Sales Group

London / New York / Paris / Sydney / Copenhagen / Berlin / Madrid / Hong Kong / Tokyo

Published by
Wise Publications
14-15 Berners Street, London W1T 3LJ, UK.

Exclusive Distributors:
Music Sales Limited
Distribution Centre, Newmarket Road,
Bury St Edmunds, Suffolk IP33 3YB, UK.
Music Sales Pty Limited
20 Resolution Drive, Caringbah, NSW 2229, Australia.

Order No. AM1002859
ISBN: 978-1-84938-976-1
This book © Copyright 2012 Wise Publications,
a division of Music Sales Limited.

Unauthorised reproduction of any part of this
publication by any means including photocopying
is an infringement of copyright.

Author: Karen Marshall.
Selected arrangements by Heather Hammond.
Project editor: Lizzie Moore.
Book design: Camden Music.
Piano played by Paul Knight.
CD mixed and mastered by Jonas Persson.
Cover design by Tim Field.
Cover photograph courtesy of Robert Kneschke - Fotolia.

Printed in the EU.

**For access to the complementary material for this book, go to
www.hybridpublications.com and enter the code GHO29.**

This book has been written in loving memory of Sarah Louise Freeman – my beautiful friend.
You are greatly missed but never forgotten. I also dedicate this book to all those adult beginner and
returners that I have worked with over the years – I have learnt so much from you all!
Thank you Heather Hammond, Christopher Walters and Lizzie Moore for your wise advice.
Thanks also to Adam (my husband) for your unfailing support and to my wonderful students for trying things out.
And finally, thank you to all my music teachers especially the late Christine Brown, a gifted teacher,
who not only taught me what to teach but how and why to teach it.

Your Guarantee of Quality
As publishers, we strive to produce every book
to the highest commercial standards.

This book has been carefully designed to minimise awkward
page turns and to make playing from it a real pleasure.

Particular care has been given to specifying acid-free, neutral-sized paper
made from pulps which have not been elemental chlorine bleached. This pulp is from
farmed sustainable forests and was produced with special regard for the environment.

Throughout, the printing and binding have been planned to ensure a sturdy,
attractive publication which should give years of enjoyment.

If your copy fails to meet our high standards, please inform us
and we will gladly replace it.

www.musicsales.com

Introduction

Congratulations on returning to the piano! This book has been put together just for you. It offers a progressive series of pieces to guide you in your journey of re-discovery with backing tracks to aid the learning process. There simply is something for everyone—pop, folk, popular, classical and film.

A number of the pieces are arrangements. These for the most part have been arranged by the composer Heather Hammond. We have worked together to ensure each piece develops different essential skills for the pianist. All are very playable and attractive; the hand is not expected to do the impossible, which is always a good thing! Having taught adults for over 20 years I know that it takes a great deal of courage to keep persevering when a piece causes difficulty. Do remember: Rome wasn't built in a day. Modern life is a fast-moving affair which can provide little time for practising the piano—little and often is best. Remember though, that the piano really is a friend worth having. You can rekindle your relationship at any time and there will always be much more pleasure to be gained.

Enjoy making music—it's a wonderful thing!

P.S. This book is merely a starting point—do look at the suggested supplementary materials (see page 60) and, if you can, find a recommended piano teacher to help you on your way.

Companion Website

This book also offers complementary bonus material. This includes some basic theory pages and a practice diary. To access this go to the book companion website at www.hybridpublications.com and enter the code GH029.

Why did you stop playing the piano?

There can be a whole range of answers to this question but here are a few solutions to problems you may have encountered in the past.

Finding playing the piano too difficult is the main one I address in various ways throughout the book, but there's also...

I was practising on a poor piano Try to get a good instrument. If you can't afford a good-quality acoustic piano then try your local music shop or visit **www.musicroom.com** for a whole range of electric pianos with authentic piano actions.

I couldn't read the music If you have a specific learning difficulty, this can (in some cases) affect one's ability to read music.

- Try putting a colour overlay over the music—you can get these cheaply from an optometrist and they stop the black/white glare.
- Enlarge the music.
- Isolate bars with 'windows' (as suggested in the book)—this helps you to process the information.
- Listen to recordings of the music and follow the score at the same time.
- Look for patterns and shapes in the notation.
- Colour code notes that you find particularly difficult to remember and circle all the sharps or flats from the key signature.

How to use this book

For adults I think there are three main factors for success. I call them the three Ps:

Patience   **P**ositivity   **P**ractice

I also have a golden rule: enjoy making music!

Take this approach, using the material in the book and you will certainly, in time, make progress. In my experience, adults often underestimate how well they are doing. The chances are that you've made much more progress than you think!

Each piece has three sections

Practice tips These provide you with a systematic way to approach the piece.

Theory This will provide you with some theoretical understanding of what you are trying to play.

Technique Here the technique required to play the piece is explained and exercises to help acquire the skills are provided on pages 61–63.

You'll also find:

- **Starting off** Hints and tips (page 6)
- **Exercises** To practise technique required to play the pieces (pages 61–63)
- **Creating your own piano curriculum** Details of books for further study (page 60)
- **Theory page** Some basic theory is available from the companion website (go to www.hybridpublications.com)

Pieces (in order of difficulty and the playing skills they develop)

- **Für Elise** Beethoven (pedalling, passing the melody through the hands)
- **Let It Be** The Beatles (for legato thirds and sixths, and arpeggiated chords)
- **Clocks** Coldplay (maintaining a constant beat)
- **The Entertainer** Joplin (rhythmic syncopation)
- **Minuet In G** J. S. Bach (Two-part playing and awareness of keyboard geography)
- **Greensleeves** Traditional (phrasing, balance and pedalling)
- **The Irish Washerwoman** Traditional (Articulation, melody moving into the left hand, rests and crossing over of the hands)
- **Theme From *Schindler's List*** John Williams (sustaining notes in the inner parts)
- **Music Box Dancer** Frank Mills (arpeggio playing, arpeggiated chords and independence of the hands)
- **The Can Can** Offenbach (articulation, finger staccato and left-hand agility)
- **Jupiter** Holst (part playing in two, three and four parts)
- **I Dreamed A Dream** Schönberg (rhythm, parallel octaves, playing an octave below and sustained notes)

Scale Shapes

The scale shapes and arpeggios you see before each piece are in the key of the piece you are about to play. You will notice some pieces are written in more than one key. Practise the relevant scales and arpeggios before playing the piece—this is great to warm up the fingers but also to get a good sense of the keys and the shapes they produce.

Starting off (hints and tips)

Posture and technique

- Check the piano stool is the right height and in the right place (not too far, or too near to the piano).

- Check you are sitting correctly—shoulders down and your back straight.

- Place your hands on your knees; maintain this shape and gently play with a relaxed hand and loose wrist on the piano keys.

Practice strategies and tools to speed up the learning process

- Study the piece before you start to play, for key (sharps and flats), timing and patterns.

- Practise slowly and gradually speed up.

- Use 'star' bars (repeated bars throughout the piece). This speeds up learning.

- Try using the idea of 'windows' for tricky bars. This means that you are only looking at one or two bars at a time. Isolating bars in this way means that you're not distracted by the whole piece, and can focus on these particular bars until you've got them right. We've marked the bars in each piece which might need this kind of attention.

- Hands separate practice is always a good idea.

- Use the *same* fingering each time you play. The tactile memory needs consistency to be accurate.

Developing sight reading skills

- Use much easier pieces to practise your reading skills (see page 15).

- Identify all the sharps and flats in the music.

- Look for patterns—arpeggio patterns or repeated melodies.

- Always look ahead—you need to know what is coming to get to the notes in time!

- Tap out the rhythm before you play the notes.

Musical communication: expression

- Think about what dynamics you are going to include. Add further dynamics within the phrases to make the music more interesting.

- Silence is important in music. Make sure the music breathes—be silent where the music suggests you should be. This is best done without the backing track.

- Think about where the music should slow down (**ritenuto, rit.**) and speed up (**accelerando, accel.**). Do this with care—it is not appropriate in the 'Minuet' by Bach, but it is very appropriate in the Theme From *Schindler's List*.

- Think about the title of the music—does your playing connect to this title? It's great to find a piece that you literally love—it provides the ideal opportunity to make music expressively!

How to best use the backing tracks

Don't get frustrated if you find playing along difficult; try to be patient.

- Listen to the backing track and just tap the pulse.

- Follow the music with your finger as you listen to the backing track.

- Slow the backing track down (using a programme from the internet such as 'Speed Shifter' from ABRSM or 'Transcribe!'). It will take lots of practise to play to a performance standard.

- Gradually speed the backing track up.

- Always keep going, perhaps missing any tricky bits at first, to ensure continuity.

Für Elise

A minor (harmonic) scale

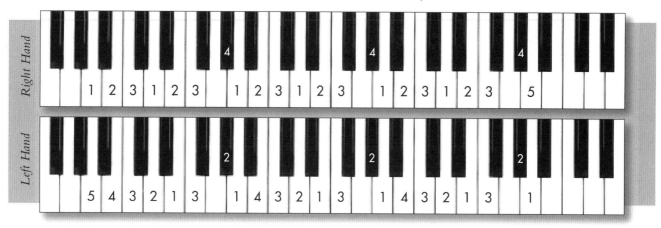

A minor arpeggio

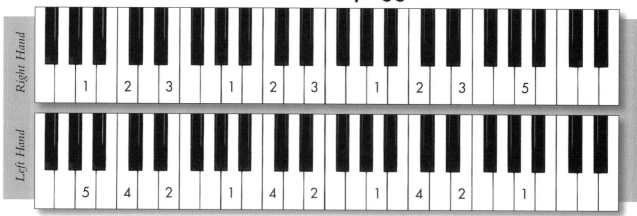

* alternative 3

PRACTICE TIPS

- Look for the repeated arpeggios in the bass—practise the five 'star bar' (★) broken chords and you will have learnt virtually all of the left hand.

- Can you work out all the repeated patterns in the right hand?

- Try to ensure that the semiquavers are played evenly, passing from one hand to the other. Practise this by playing on the wooden lid of the piano; your taps need to be even.

- Play the right hand only, and then the left hand only, with the backing track. Put the pedal in with the left-hand practice. Change the pedal with every chord, making sure there is no blurring.

- Listen out to make sure you play this in $\frac{3}{8}$ rather than $\frac{6}{16}$. To do this, try not to stress the fourth semiquaver in the bar, but the first and fifth.

- Window bars 13, 14, 15 and 16—make sure you don't put in extra notes and that you use your left hand in the treble clef (where your right hand normally plays).

Theory

- The curved lines above all the notes are **phrase marks**. This means all the notes underneath the mark need to be joined together, without a break.

- Notice the little **sharp signs** (♯)—these are accidentals (additional changed notes that are not in the key signature). The note needs to stay *sharp* for the entire bar unless you see the **natural sign** (♮) (see bar 1—the D is *sharpened*, then a *natural* sign appears in front of the next D, meaning play D♮).

- Here is a list of the Italian terms used in this piece of music and their meanings:

    pp (**pianissimo**): very quiet

    mf (**mezzo forte**): moderately loud

    dim. or ⟩————⟨ : gradually get quieter

    cresc. or ⟨————⟩ : gradually get louder

    rit. : gradually get slower

    A tempo: in time (return to the original speed)

Technique

- Practise:

    Exercise 1 (page 61) for flexible wrist

    Exercise 3 (page 62) for legato

    Exercise 6 (page 63) for a flat lateral wrist movement and pedalling

- This piece demands a flexible lateral wrist movement in both hands, to produce a smooth (**legato**) effect where the melody passes from one hand to the other.

Für Elise

Music by Ludwig Van Beethoven

© Copyright 2012 Dorsey Brothers Music Limited.
All Rights Reserved. International Copyright Secured.

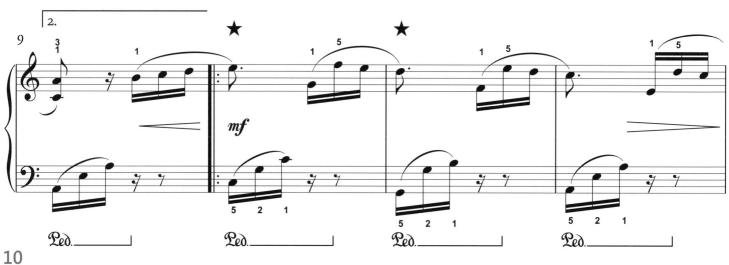

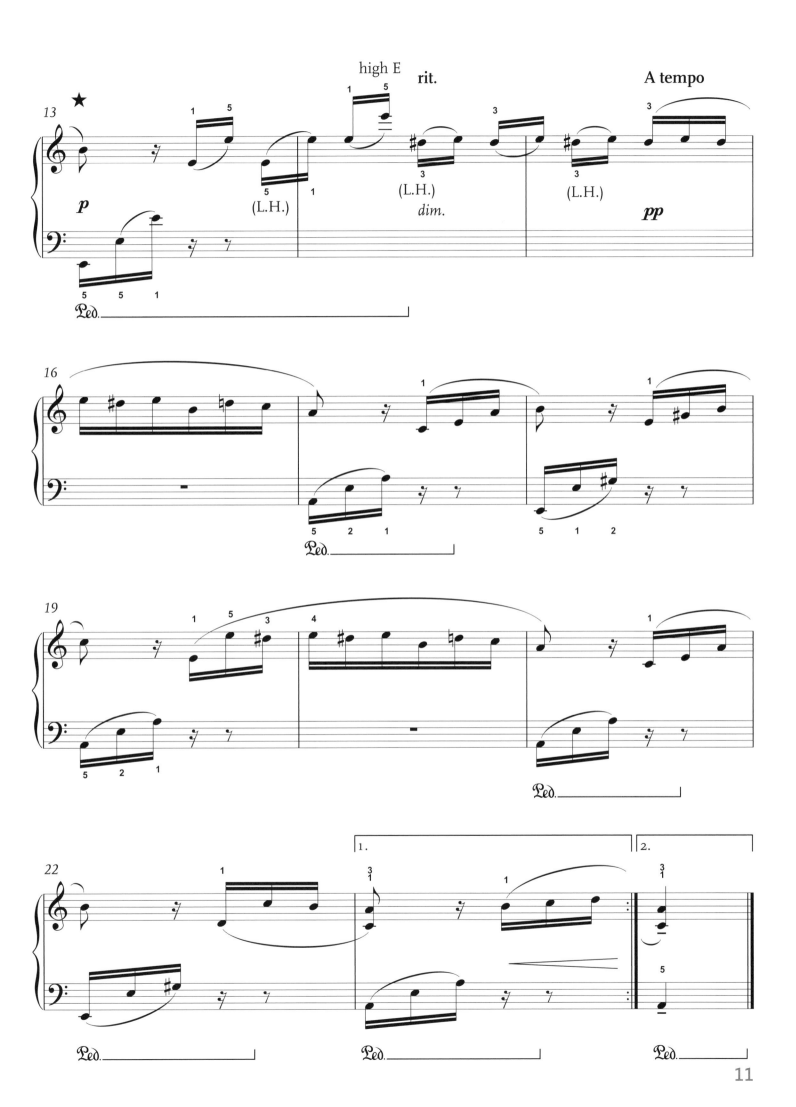

Let It Be

F major scale

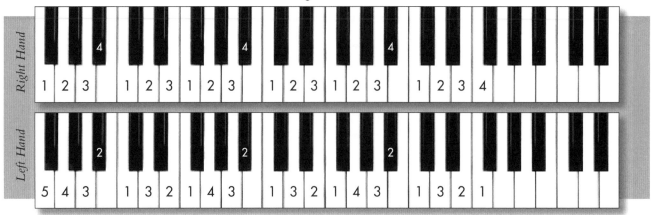

F major arpeggio

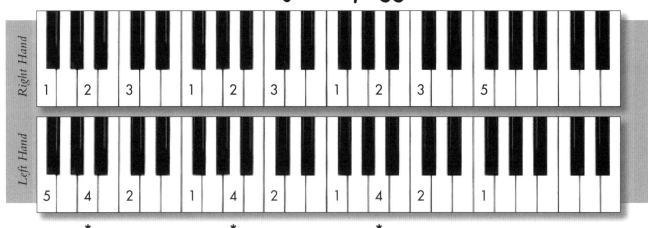

* alternative 3

PRACTICE TIPS

- Note that bars 3 and 4 (star bars) are repeated an octave higher in bars 7 and 8. Can you see which other bars are repeated?

- Play the hands separately to ensure you hold all the notes for their full value (bar 10 is particularly tricky; window this bar). Use the backing track to practise each part individually.

- Practise the arpeggiated chords in bars 15 and 16, firstly as solid chords then separately from low to high as a quick roll of the hand.

- Practise the pedal—two per bar except for bars where the harmony changes. Example bars: 6 and 15, where each chord should be separately pedalled.

Theory

- Legato *thirds* and *sixths*—we describe two notes played at the same time by the distance between each other.
  Bar 4: first two right-hand notes—these are thirds
  Bar 9: first two right-hand notes—these are sixths

  3rd: line to line, or space to space   **6th:** four notes in between

- Notice the $\mathbf{C}$ in place of the time signature. This represents **common time**, which is the same as $\frac{4}{4}$ (four crotchets in a bar).

- The piece is in **F major**. The key of the piece is identified at the beginning of the music by seeing which sharps or flats are indicated. The B♭ indicates this is F major (see the circle of 5ths on the theory pages of the companion website).

- Here is a list of the Italian terms and symbols used in this piece of music and their meanings:

  p (**piano**): quiet
  mp (**mezzo piano**): moderately quiet
  mf (**mezzo forte**): moderately loud
  cresc. **:** gradually get louder
  dim. **:** gradually get quieter
  ⌢ **:** pause

Technique

- Arpeggiated chords should be played with a loose rotary wrist action.

- Practise:

  Exercise 2 for the thirds and sixths making sure they are played with a loose wrist and the notes are clearly joined. Take care to use the correct fingering.
  Exercise 6 for pedalling and the arpeggiated chords. Try to create a clean sound using the right pedal (damper pedal). Change the pedal when the harmony changes.
  Exercise 5 to practise part-playing. See the second bullet point under *Practice tips*.

Let It Be

Words & Music by John Lennon & Paul McCartney

© Copyright 1970 Sony/ATV Music Publishing.
All Rights Reserved. International Copyright Secured.

Sight reading

Here are a few sight reading examples to have a go at. Remember to check the key and time signature before playing. Tapping out the rhythm first and hands separate practice also helps. Try reading a little ahead, even if it's just a beat ahead. Avoid correcting yourself—just keep going!

Clocks

D major arpeggio

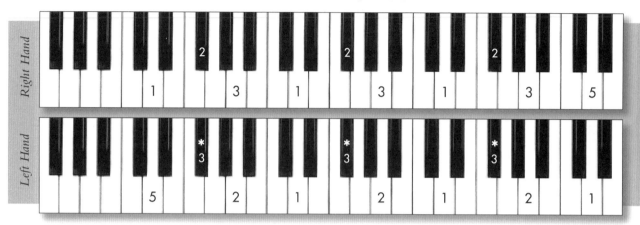

* alternative 4

A minor arpeggio

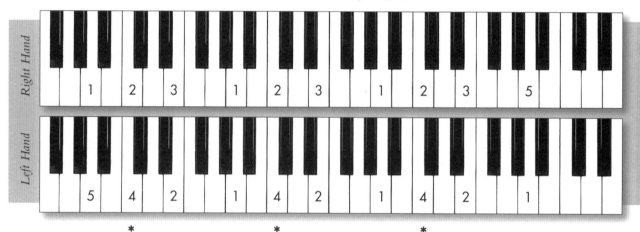

* alternative 3

E minor arpeggio

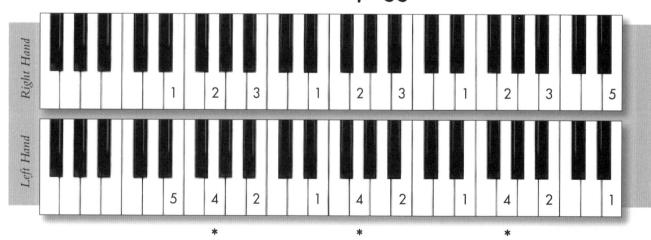

* alternative 3

PRACTICE TIPS

- Practise the broken chords at the beginning (for details see theory notes below) as solid chords, and then break them up when confident. Make sure the notes are even, using the piano lid again.
- To ensure the rhythm is correct, count quavers instead of crotchets (see theory page for details of note values). This means counting eight in a bar:

- Can you find all the repeated bars and practise them?
- Split the music and learn it in three sections: A (bars 1–8), B (9–24) and C (25 to the end). Note that bar 29 onwards is a repeat of the beginning.
- Take care with the rests used in bars 25 and 27.

Theory

- A chord **triad** is made up of three notes—the first, third and fifth note that appears in the key's scale. C major includes the notes C D E F G A B C. We use C E G for the **tonic triad** (**root position**).
- We can change the tonic triad into **first** and **second inversion** chords:

  C E G becomes **E** G C (for the first inversion) and **G** C E (for the second inversion). Notice that the first note in the first inversion is the second note of the tonic triad and the second inversion starts on the third note of the tonic triad.

  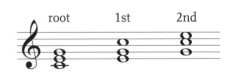

- In 'Clocks', three triads are used. The first is a D major tonic triad in first inversion; the second is in A minor in second inversion; the final chord is the tonic triad of E minor in root position.

Technique

- Think about the title, 'Clocks'. Try to make the repeated notes in the bass a tick in the background. To do this, lightly stress the first beat, but do not let your thumb be too heavy.
- There is an **ostinato** (repeated pattern) used throughout the main verse—F♯, E, E, D. Make sure you sustain these semibreves throughout the bar as the melody sounds above.
- Practise:
    Exercise 3 for legato and staccato
    Exercise 5 for part playing
    Exercise 6 for chords and arpeggios

Clocks

Words & Music by Guy Berryman, Chris Martin, Jon Buckland & Will Champion

© Copyright 2003 Universal Music Publishing MGB Limited.
All Rights in Germany Administered by Musik Edition Discoton GmbH (A Division of Universal Music Publishing Group).
All Rights Reserved. International Copyright Secured.

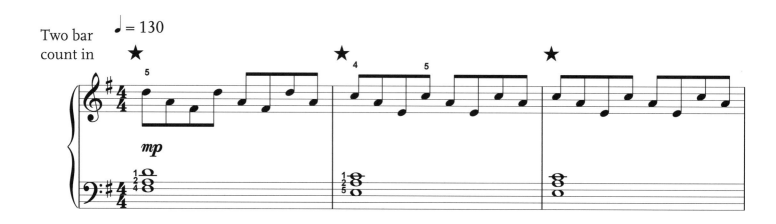

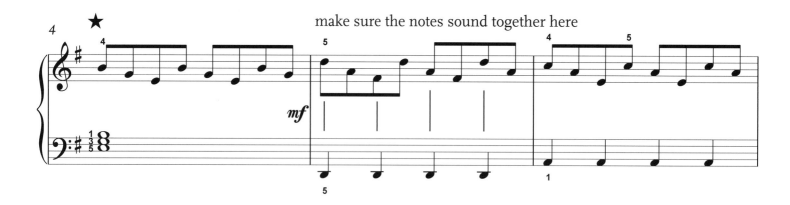

make sure the notes sound together here

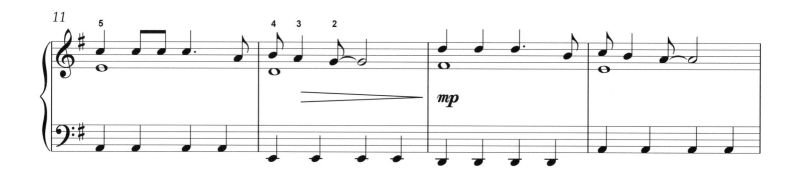

The Entertainer

C major scale

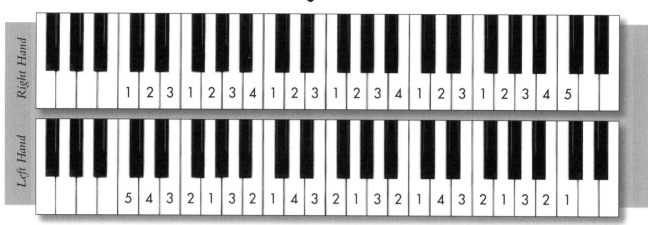

C major arpeggio

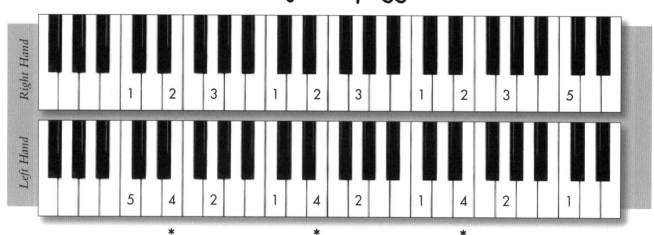

* alternative 3

PRACTICE TIPS

- Start by simply clapping the pulse of the piece, four beats per bar, to the backing track. Repeat this by splitting the pulse to eight quavers per bar.

- Counting quavers, clap the rhythm of the right-hand part with the backing track. Make sure all the ties (see theory note opposite) and rests are observed.

- Clap the rhythm of the right hand on the right knee and left hand on the left knee. Then play each part separately on the piano.

- Difficult bars requiring windows are 6, 7, 11, 23, 24, 26 and 27.

Theory

- A **tie** joins two notes of the same pitch together. This means you need to hold the note for the length of both note values. For example, two quavers become a crotchet. This is used to increase note lengths over the bar or across note groupings.

- The rhythm of the music is **syncopated**. This means that the stressed notes appear off the beat. This has been achieved by using ties and quaver, crotchet, quaver rhythm patterns.

- Here is a list of the Italian terms used in this piece of music and their meanings:

    mf : moderately loud

    f : loud

    mp : moderately quiet

    cresc. : gradually get louder

- Normally the stress appears on the first and third beat in $\frac{4}{4}$ time—not here though, making the music *syncopated*.

- Notice also the articulation signs:

    Staccato (♩)**:** short detached; **Accent** (♩): with force; **Tenuto** (♩): weight mark

- When two different pitched notes are joined together with a phrase mark this is called a *couplet slur*.

- **D.S. al Fine:** go back to the sign 𝄋 and finish at the **Fine**.

Technique

- Focus on the articulation, making sure you play all the slurs, phrase marks, staccato, accents and tenuto signs that are marked in the music.
- Practise:

    Exercise 2 for thirds and sixths

    Exercise 3 for legato, staccato and accents

    Exercise 6 for arpeggios and chords

The Entertainer

Music by Scott Joplin

© Copyright 2012 Dorsey Brothers Music Limited.
All Rights Reserved. International Copyright Secured.

Minuet In G

G major scale

G major arpeggio

* alternative 3

PRACTICE TIPS

- Notice this piece is mainly written in two parts—the treble and bass. Play each part separately (with correct fingering) alongside the backing track.

- Silently touch the notes without sounding them, each hand separately. Make sure in bar 3 the hand squeezes together from E to C using fifth and first fingers. Take special note of all the new hand positions (for example, bar 17).

- Difficult bars to use a window over: 3, 7, 15, 19 and 20, 25, 26 (take care with sustained notes here).

Theory

- A **minuet** is a dance in 3-time. This particular one was written for Bach's *Anna Magdalena Notebook*—a collection of pieces by Bach and his students to teach his second wife, Anna, to play the clavier (an early keyboard instrument).
  This piece, which is mainly attributed to Bach, was actually written by his pupil Christian Petzold.

- The piece **modulates** (changes key) from G major to D major in bar 20. We know this because of the introduction of the C♯.

- Notice the *tonic triad* chord of G major in the left hand, bar 1.

- Can you remember what all the Italian terms mean from the other pieces? *Allegretto*, the mark at the beginning of the piece, is the tempo mark (what speed to play)—meaning 'lively'.

Technique

- Try to ensure that the phrasing is clearly marked.
  Practise the legato and staccato **Exercise 3**.

- Practise **Exercise 1b** for the couplet slur. Although the slurs here use more than two notes, practising the 'float off' is really helpful.

- Ensure all notes of the chord sound at the same time and dynamic.
  Practise with the arpeggio/chord **Exercise 6**.

- Make sure all sustained notes are held. Use **Exercise 5** for part-playing.

Minuet In G

Composed by Johann Sebastian Bach

© Copyright 2012 Dorsey Brothers Music Limited.
All Rights Reserved. International Copyright Secured.

cross 2nd finger
over thumb

new hand position

new hand position

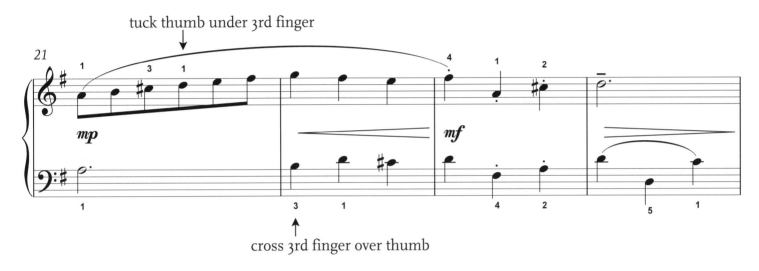

tuck thumb under 3rd finger

cross 3rd finger over thumb

hold for two beats each

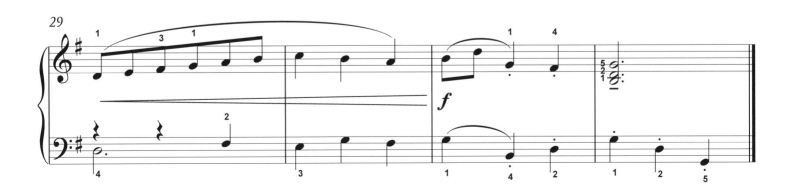

Greensleeves

A minor (melodic) scale, up and down

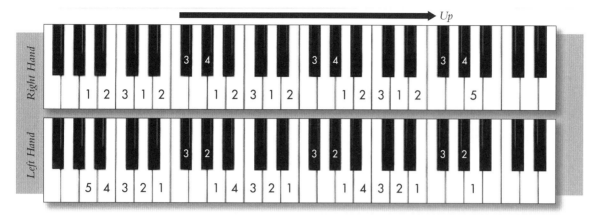

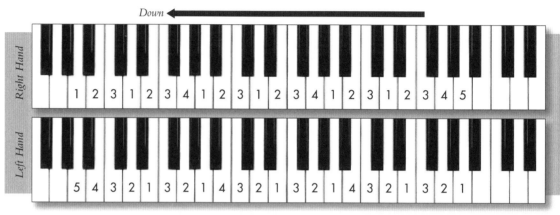

A minor (harmonic) scale

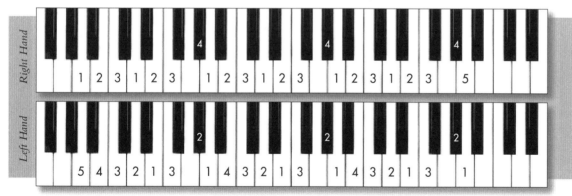

PRACTICE TIPS

- Window bars: 8, 16, 20 (make sure you play the dotted rhythm correctly) and 33 (sustain the parts).

- You can use words to help you play rhythms correctly. Try 'gra - cious queen' here:

28

> ## MORE PRACTICE TIPS
>
> - The entire left-hand part on the first page is based on seven arpeggio patterns (practise as star bars individually). Use the fingering given. Take great care to mark the phrasing and not to bang the thumb.
>
> - Add in the pedal with the harmony, one pedal per bar.

Theory

- This arrangement is written using the notes of the A **melodic minor** scale. The notes of this scale are different depending upon whether you are going up or down:

    Ascending A B C D E F♯ G♯ A
    Descending A G F E D C B A

    Coming down, the sixth and seventh notes become natural again, lowering a semitone. This is also called the **natural minor**.

- There is another minor scale, the **harmonic minor**. This scale is: A B C D E F G♯ A.

- Notice the pause mark at the end (⌢). This means to hold the note for longer (perhaps up to double the length).

Technique

- Warm up with the arpeggio **Exercise 6**. When you practise the left hand, try using a flatter hand and a lateral wrist. Use this to practise pedalling as well.

- Bar 19 requires a rotary wrist action, gentle rocking on the broken chords. **Exercise 1** helps with this.

Creative opportunity: improvisation

Improvisation means spontaneous composition: inventing your own tune on the spot. Why not have a go at improvising using the *A melodic minor scale*. Using the notes from the scale, string together a few notes, firstly using notes next to each other, then perhaps a third apart. Try two phrases: a question tune then an answer tune. Experiment with the backing CD to see what melodies fit with the harmony of the music.

Greensleeves

Traditional

© Copyright 2012 Dorsey Brothers Music Limited.
All Rights Reserved. International Copyright Secured.

The Irish Washerwoman

G major scale

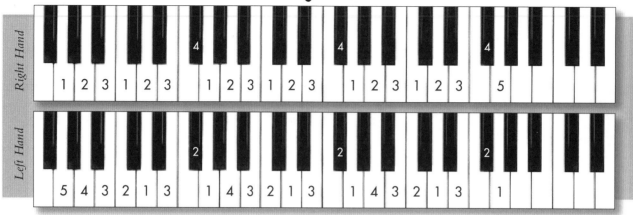

G major arpeggio

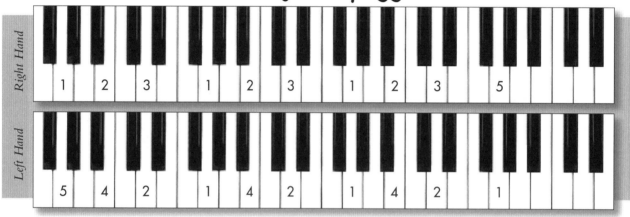

* alternative 3

PRACTICE TIPS

- Can you tap six beats as you listen to the backing track, then just two, marking each dotted crotchet?

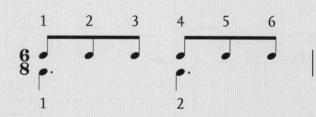

- Play the right hand separately, ensuring all the articulation is clearly marked—couplet slurs, staccato, phrase marks and accents.

- Practise bars 19–24 as window bars. Practise the left hand only (without the right hand) to correctly place the chords (thirds) that sound below the right-hand part.

- Listen to the backing track and clap where all the rests appear in the right hand. Then play the right hand on the piano, making sure all the rests are properly marked.

Theory

- **$\frac{6}{8}$ time.** The **8** at the bottom of the time signature indicates that you are counting quaver beats. If it were **4**, that would mean you would count crotchet beats.

  Notice that in the left hand there are lots of dotted crotchets. $\frac{6}{8}$ is also referred to as **compound duple time**.

  Compound time includes 6, 9 and 12 beats in a bar. The 'duple' refers to the fact that the music can be marked by the two dotted crotchet beats in a bar.

  Here are some examples of different rhythmic configurations in compound duple time:

Technique

- Play with a loose wrist, making sure the hand drops on the first of each couplet slur and lifts on the second. Practise with **Exercise 1b**. Try to 'kick off' the second note.

- Use **Exercise 3** to practise a crisp finger staccato.

- Get the left hand to frog-jump over the right arm and very lightly play the staccato thirds (use **Exercise 4**).

- Use vertical wrist action to play the sixths in bar 18 (see **Exercise 2b**, playing the staccato sixths).

Creative opportunity: playing by ear

Listen to the backing track and try to play it from memory. Take notice of all the finger patterns, interval jumps and repeated phrases. Work on these in small, manageable chunks.

The Irish Washerwoman

Traditional

© Copyright 2012 Dorsey Brothers Music Limited.
All Rights Reserved. International Copyright Secured.

Music Box Dancer

C major scale

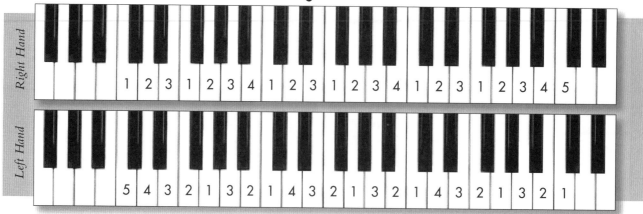

C major arpeggio

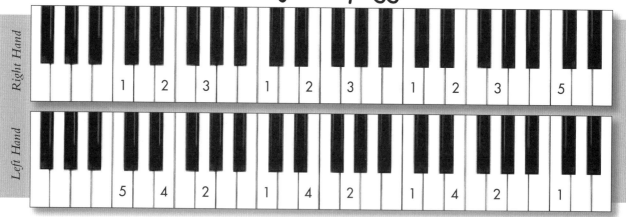

* alternative 3

PRACTICE TIPS

- Much of this piece is comprised of repeated patterns. The first nine-bar section is almost identically repeated again from bar 18 to the end. Practise the two *A sections* (bars 1–9, 18–25) first, then look at the *B section* (bars 10–17).

- Play the right-hand and left-hand broken chord patterns as solid chords.

- I suggest to window bars 10, 11 and 13. These are tricky to coordinate so do take care over them.

- Practise the hands separately to get the right-hand legato and the left-hand staccato. Try this at the same time on your knees, feeling the little stabs of the left hand and smoothness of the right hand. Be patient; achieving this on the piano can be very difficult.

- Notice that the right hand moves up the octave for a few bars: 5, 12, 16 and 21. Check where you are moving to first.

Theory

- The term *8ᵛᵃ* means 'play an octave higher' and *loco* means 'at normal pitch' (so move back down the octave).

- **Poco rit.** means a little slower. The ¢ symbol is a time signature and means the same as $\frac{2}{2}$. It means **split common time**.

Technique

- Practise **Exercise 3** for independence of the hands and different touches (staccato and legato).

- The arpeggios in the right hand and left hand require a flat lateral wrist movement. Use **Exercise 6** for this.

Music Box Dancer

Music by Frank Mills

© Copyright 1974 North Country Music Limited, Canada.
Valentine Music Group Limited.
All Rights Reserved. International Copyright Secured.

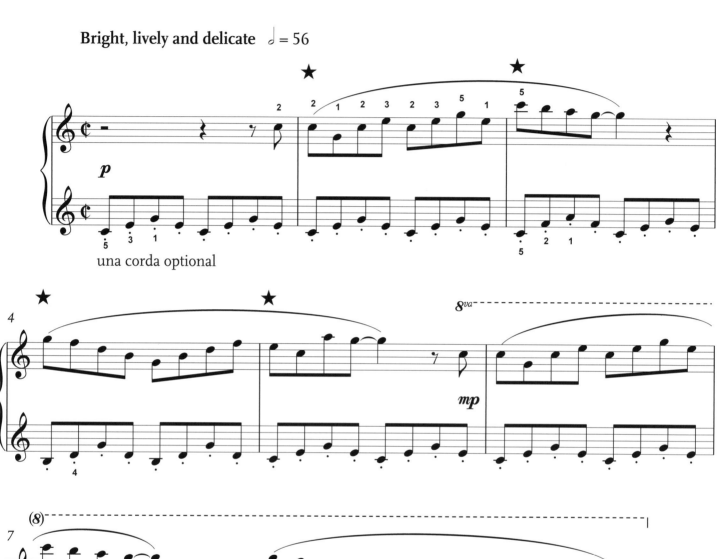

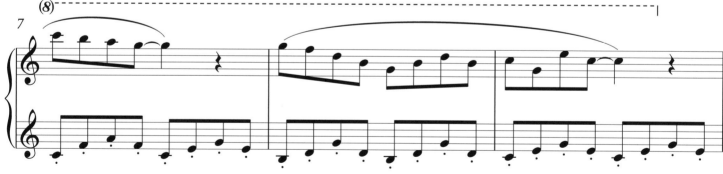

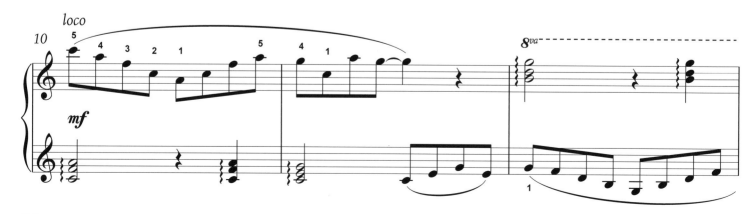

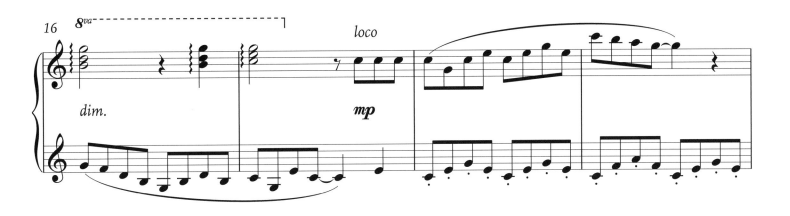

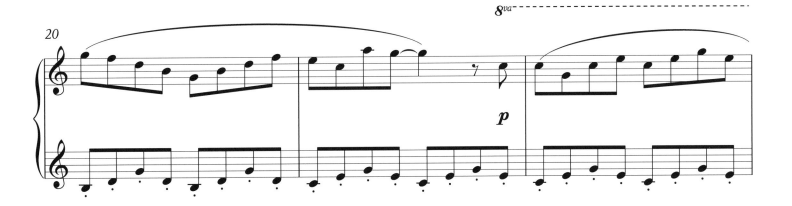

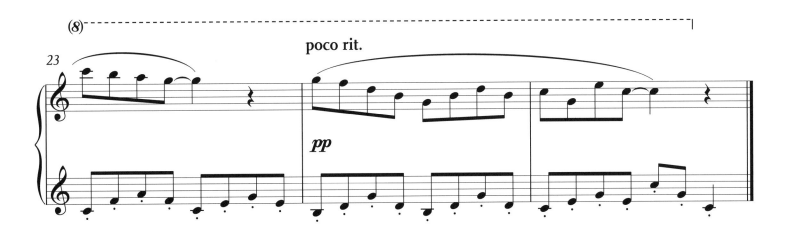

The Can Can

C major scale and arpeggio

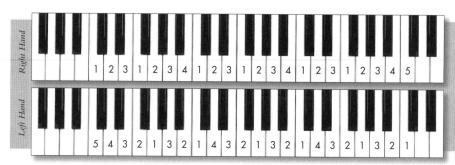

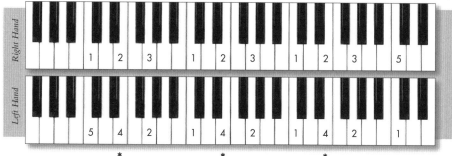

* alternative 3

G major scale and arpeggio

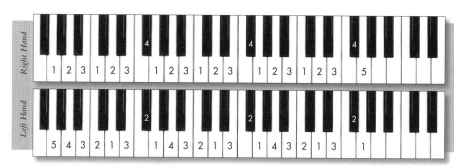

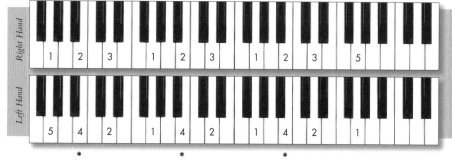

* alternative 3

PRACTICE TIPS

- Learn the left hand first. A lot of this is repeated so make sure you have it under your fingers. This then leaves you to concentrate on the tune in the right hand. Gradually increase the speed of your practice. This is really quite a workout for the left hand.

- Notice that many bars are repeated. Try practising in sections beginning with bars 1–18, then bars 19–34, and finally bars 35–56.
  The rest of the music is repeated but in a different key—what is it?

- Play each individual part, right hand and left hand, with the backing CD. Make sure you put in all the articulation (slurs, accents and staccatos) and the rests.

ANOTHER PRACTICE TIP

- Bar 19 onwards (left hand) is particularly tricky: it's a total workout. Play these bars separately and slowly. Don't strain your hand. If tightness appears, stop immediately. Check your shoulders are down and relaxed and that you are sitting straight, with good posture.

Theory

- Notice the whole bar rests in bars 1 and 2.
- The music changes key in bar 35 to G major, so remember to use F♯. This is the *dominant key* of C major; the dominant refers to the fifth note of the scale.
- The structure of the music is **ternary**; this means there are three main sections.
- Notice that the piece includes lots of different intervals.

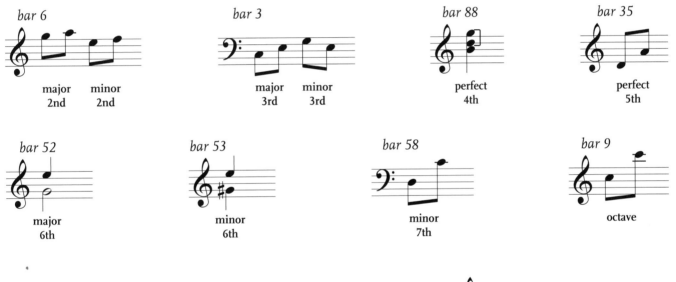

There is no augmented 4th which would look like this:

Or major 7th which would look like this:

Technique

- Again, independence of the hands is required, with the right-hand articulation differing to the left hand. Practise the different touches again away from the keys (on the lid) and use **Exercise 3**.
- There are couplet slurs in various intervals, which also can be large leaps in the right hand or left hand. Use **Exercise 1a** and **1b** to help here.
- Use **Exercise 2** for the accented sixth in the right hand from bar 47, staccato and legato.

The Can Can

Music by Jacques Offenbach

© Copyright 2012 Dorsey Brothers Music Limited.
All Rights Reserved. International Copyright Secured.

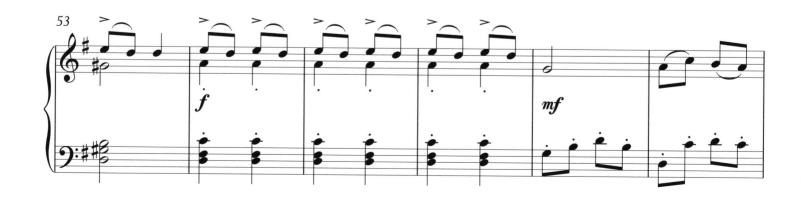

Theme From Schindler's List

C minor (harmonic) scale

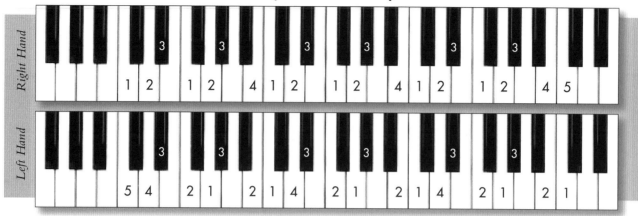

C minor arpeggio

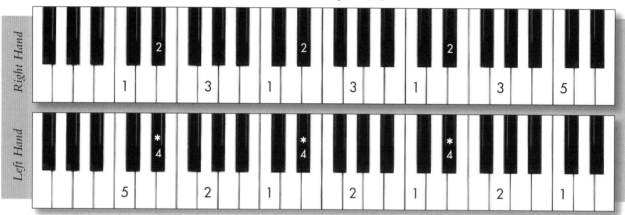

PRACTICE TIPS

- This piece demands meticulous observation to ensure the parts are correctly sustained. Go through and take note of all the sustained notes in the right and left hands. Window these bars: 6, 7, 8, 9, 11, 20, 21, 22, 23, 25 and 27.

- Bars 15–18 are rhythmically challenging. Listen to these bars on the backing track and clap four beats (marking crotchets), then eight beats (marking quavers) and finally 16 beats (marking semiquavers—four claps per crotchet beat). This will help you break down the rhythm and play the semiquavers in the correct time.

bar 15, counting in semiquavers...

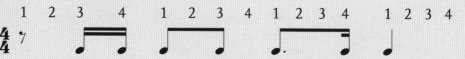

MORE PRACTICE TIPS

- Find the repeated bars and choose your own star bars.

- Take care with the key signatures (see explanation below) and all the accidentals (lots of B♮s). B♭s are also re-introduced at times, and do look out for the rogue F♯.

- If you like singing, try singing the melody with the backing track (an octave lower) to get the feel of the phrasing. One phrase usually means one breath. As you play this on the piano try to make the whole phrase legato.

- Balance—remember the left hand needs to be much quieter, for the most part, than the right hand, which is the melody. Practise playing on the piano lid pushing harder on the wood for the right hand, focusing on what that feels like. Be patient—getting one hand *mf* and the other *p* is a real challenge and takes time!

Theory

- The music is in three flats, but the key is not E♭ major—it is C minor. This is the **relative minor** of E♭ major. We know this because of the number of B♮s and by listening to the music, which sounds sad.

- Notice all the different kinds of rests:

| quaver | crotchet | minim | whole bar |

Technique

- Practise:
    Exercise 5 for part playing
    Exercise 3b for balance (right hand *mf*, left hand *mp*)
    Exercise 2 for legato thirds and sixths
    Exercise 6 for flat lateral wrist movement to play the arpeggio patterns.

- Take great care with the fingering to ensure the part playing is accurate.

- Pedal with the harmony—two pedals per bar, and then continue to follow the harmony.

Theme From Schindler's List

Music by John Williams

© Copyright 1993 Music Corporation Of America Incorporated, USA.
Universal/MCA Music Limited.
All rights in Germany administered by Universal/MCA Music Publ. GmbH.
All Rights Reserved. International Copyright Secured.

Jupiter

F major scale

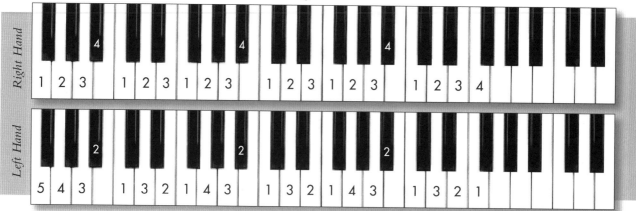

F major arpeggio

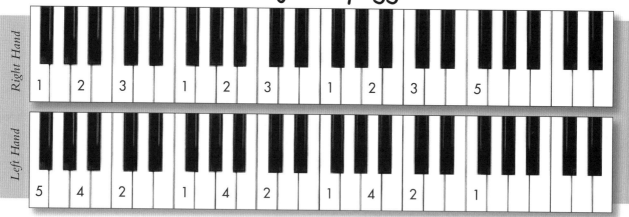

* alternative 3

PRACTICE TIPS

- This piece has been written purposely in two-part, three-part and then full four-part harmony to develop your part-playing. First of all, can you identify all the different parts? It may help to highlight them in different colour pencils.

- Follow the fingering meticulously (even add your own) as you play the parts—this is essential to ensure the legato phrasing. Remember, you can hold down just one of the notes of a chord, *not* all three if it's too difficult. **Practise without the pedal to ensure you are playing legato and not using the pedal to do the job instead!**

- Window bars—I'd recommend that you window bars 21 and 25–28 (for those left-hand octaves) and 36 to the end as it's all rather difficult!

- Practise all the parts individually with the backing CD, then the right hand only, left hand only and finally combine the two parts together. Put the pedal in to check that there is no blurring and that you are changing the pedal with the harmony.

Theory

- This piece is great for learning more about harmony. The piece is in F major and the chords in F major are as follows:

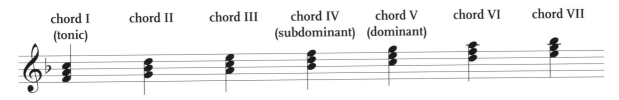

- Chords I, IV and V are really important chords—we call them *primary chords*. The entire scale can be harmonised using just these three chords. Why not try it in the key of F major:

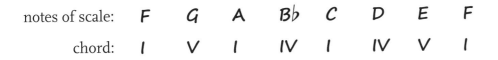

- We use these chords to form **cadences**. A *cadence* is made up of two chords at the end of a phrase. There are four different kinds of cadence:

  Two that sound finished: **perfect** (chords V to I) and **plagal** (chords IV to I)
  Two that sound unfinished: **imperfect** (any chord going to V) and **interrupted** (chords V to VI).

- Examples of three of these cadences in the music:

  Perfect: Last bar—can you see how chord V has changed? A B♭ (the minor 7th note in the chord) has been added as well as the C to turn this dominant chord into a **dominant 7th**.
  Imperfect: bar 13, last beat and the first two beats of bar 14.
  Interrupted: bar 23, last chord and first chord of bar 24.

Technique

- Practise:

  Exercise 5 for part playing
  Exercise 6 for chords and pedalling

- Try to make sure all the notes of the chord sound together and legato is maintained throughout the phrases.

Jupiter

Music by Gustav Holst

© Copyright 1921 Goodwin & Tabb Limited.
Transferred to J. Curwen & Sons Limited.
All Rights Reserved. International Copyright Secured.

Andante maestoso ♩ = 88–96

I Dreamed A Dream

Eb major scale
and arpeggio

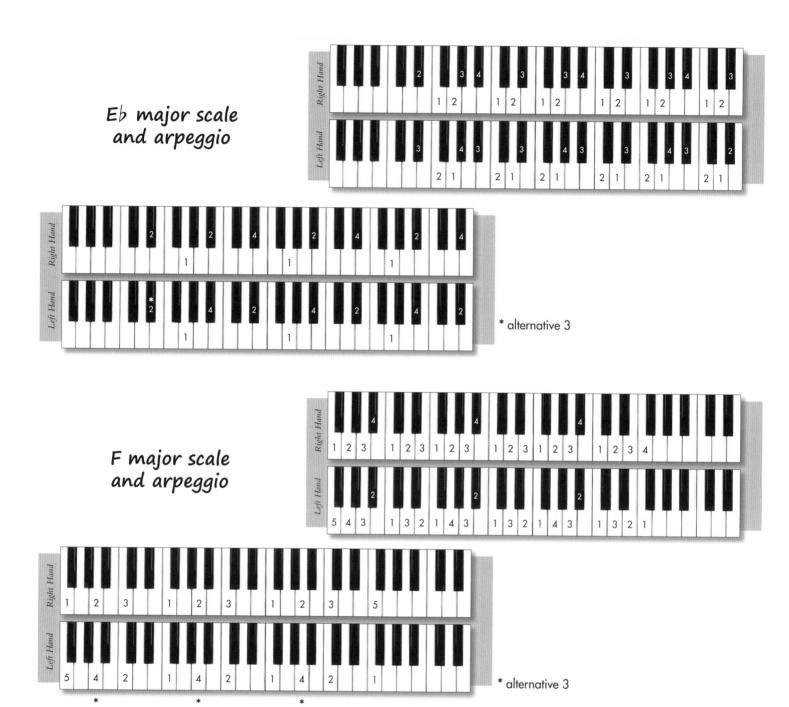

F major scale
and arpeggio

* alternative 3

* alternative 3

Well done! You have reached the final piece of music. This piece is much harder than anything else you've played so far in this book. It may, at this point, be 'a bit of a dream' to play it. A difficult goal that, if approached with tenacity and the right methods, can be achieved. Use everything you have learnt so far to tackle this beautiful arrangement of a well-loved song. The important thing is to simply enjoy playing it.

As I've already said, making music is a wonderful thing. Good luck, as hopefully you will go on to make much more!

PRACTICE TIPS

- Play the left hand only with the backing track, counting the rhythm in quavers. Once the left-hand rhythm is secure use this to work out the right-hand rhythm.

- Watch out for the right-hand rests in bars 11, 25 and 38. In bars 13 and 17 the right hand needs to move out of the way quite quickly.

- Ensure all the held notes are sustained throughout the bars. Notice the left-hand minims from bars 4–18 and later in the music; also the semibreves in the right hand (middle C bars 6 and 10).

- Watch out for the left-hand rhythm in bar 19; window this bar. Count the quavers and make sure the right hand plays clearly in the quaver rest before the left hand sounds. Bar 29 is similar but with a different left-hand rhythm—make sure you play the new rhythms correctly.

- The triplets in bars 39–41 can be worked out by clapping a $\frac{12}{8}$ rhythm to the backing track (see below). A similar exercise works well for semiquavers.

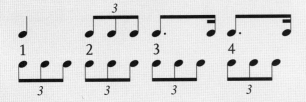

- Window bars 42, 43, 44 and 45 for the left-hand octaves (use **Exercise 2** to help here).

Theory

- Notice the key modulates from E♭ major to F major in bar 31.

- The 8vb means to play an octave lower.

- Notice all the ledger line notes (these are the notes off the stave)—see the low G in bar 38.

Technique

- Practise:
    Exercise 2 for octaves (try alternating the 4th and 5th finger to achieve a better legato)
    Exercise 3 for cantabile legato
    Exercise 5 for detailed part playing
    Exercise 6 for arpeggio work needing a flat lateral wrist

I Dreamed A Dream

Music by Claude-Michel Schönberg
Original Lyrics by Alain Boublil & Jean-Marc Natel, English Lyrics by Herbert Kretzmer

© Copyright (Music & Lyrics) 1980 Editions Musicales Alain Boublil.
English Lyrics © Copyright 1985 Alain Boublil Music Limited.
All Rights Reserved. International Copyright Secured.

Andante espressivo ♩ = 80

rit.   A tempo

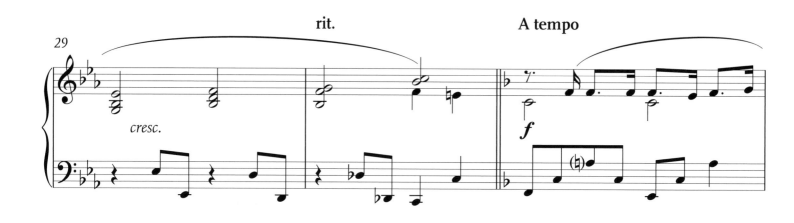

cresc.   f

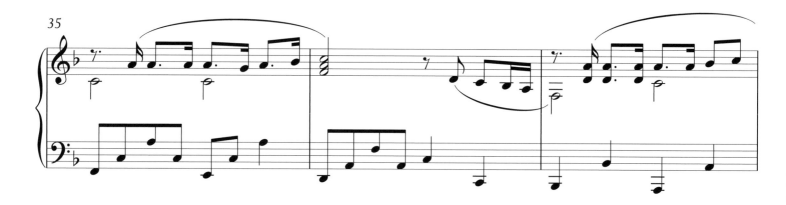

What next? Creating your own curriculum

Here are some suggestions for further Music Sales publications to help you continue to progress with the piano:

Sight reading

Do this daily—better reading increases your ability to learn new material much faster. Practise with the backing track so that you are forced to keep going and look ahead. Suggested materials for practising sight reading include:

- **Easiest 5-Finger Piano Collection** (*Wise Publications*)

  This works as good sight reading practice as the music is simple to read and therefore encourages you to look ahead to what's coming before you play. This series also has piano duet accompaniments if you can find someone to play along!

- **Sight Reading Success** (*Rhinegold Education*)

  This sight reading tutor is a systematic approach to developing all the key skills needed for this method of practice. It covers key awareness, memorising, looking ahead and rhythm.

Theory

- **How To Crack Music Theory** (*Wise Publications*)

  It's great to understand what you are playing. Use this book as part of your piano practice. It is written in plain English with a minimum of jargon and is supplemented by audio material, additional worksheets and tests on the complementary website.

There are also some basic theory pages available on the book companion website at www.hybridpublications.com.

Technique

Scales develop a wide range of skills useful to the pianist. These include key awareness, learning the geography of the keyboard and increasing finger agility and evenness.

- **Scales Shapes** (*Chester Music*)

  Use a simple scale manual. These books by Fredrick Stocken have been a real lifeline to some of my students, especially the ones with dyslexia. The grade 5 book has all the keys included and students love the diagrams of the keyboard rather than the mass of notes. They can focus on the patterns and see where the correct fingers need to go.

More Repertoire

Now that you've started playing, it's important to keep going. Try to buy a selection of books that are easy, manageable and perhaps just one that's a challenge. Again, don't take on too much to begin with as you might become discouraged. Do try to attend some live performances to inspire ideas for new pieces you would like to play and composer's music to source.

Exercises

These exercises are short and easy to read so you can focus on the technique being developed rather than learning the notes. Always start by practising slowly, making sure the hands are relaxed, use consistent fingering and sit correctly.

1 Rocking

a Developing the rotary wrist movement (like turning a door knob)

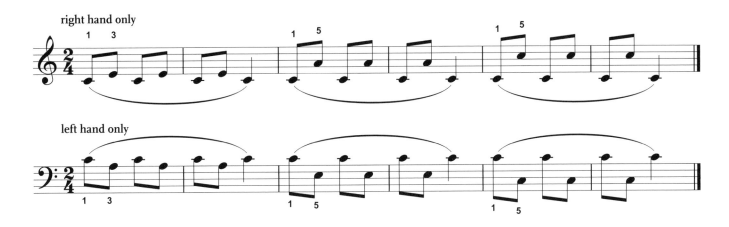

b Drop down and float off (playing couplet slurs)

The same notes as above are used but the articulation has changed. The second note can 'kick off' or 'float off' depending on the style of the music. A flexible wrist is required to drop on the first note of the slur and lift off the second note.

2 Playing legato thirds, sixths and octaves

a Try to follow the fingering, playing with a loose wrist. Play hands separately until confident.

b Why not try the sixths and octaves staccato (the wrist is loose — drops and then springs back)

3 Legato and staccato

a Try this exercise in this order:

- Both parts legato
- Both parts staccato
- Right hand legato and left hand staccato
- Left hand legato and right hand staccato

b Now try changing the dynamics like this:

- Both parts quiet ($\boldsymbol{p}$)
- Both parts loud ($\boldsymbol{f}$)
- Right hand quiet and left hand loud
- Left hand quiet and right hand loud

4 Crossing left hand over right hand

Add the damper pedal (right pedal), holding the pedal for a bar each time.

5 Part playing

Keep the notes held for their full value. Play just one part at a time to begin with, for example, the dotted minims of the bass part (bottom C–G–G–C).

6 Arpeggios and chords

A flatter hand and flatter fingers (further up the keys) can help when playing arpeggios, gently swaying the wrist from side to side (lateral wrist movement). Make sure all the notes of the solid chords are pressed at the same time and with the same dynamic.

Try to follow the fingering—it's tricky but well worth doing. First try it legato without the pedal, and then try with the pedal.

3 4 5 6 7 8 9

RESTART PIANO CD TRACK LISTING

FULL INSTRUMENTAL PERFORMANCES

1. FÜR ELISE
(BEETHOVEN)
DORSEY BROTHERS MUSIC LIMITED

2. LET IT BE
(LENNON/McCARTNEY)
SONY/ATV MUSIC PUBLISHING (UK) LIMITED

3. CLOCKS
(BERRYMAN/MARTIN/BUCKLAND/CHAMPION)
UNIVERSAL MUSIC PUBLISHING MGB LIMITED

4. THE ENTERTAINER
(JOPLIN)
DORSEY BROTHERS MUSIC LIMITED

5. MINUET IN G
(BACH)
DORSEY BROTHERS MUSIC LIMITED

6. GREENSLEEVES
(TRADITIONAL)
DORSEY BROTHERS MUSIC LIMITED

7. THE IRISH WASHERWOMAN
(TRADITIONAL)
DORSEY BROTHERS MUSIC LIMITED

8. MUSIC BOX DANCER
(MILLS)
VALENTINE MUSIC GROUP LIMITED

9. THE CAN CAN
(OFFENBACH)
DORSEY BROTHERS MUSIC LIMITED

10. THEME FROM *SCHINDLER'S LIST*
(WILLIAMS)
UNIVERSAL/MCA MUSIC LIMITED

11. JUPITER
(HOLST)
DORSEY BROTHERS MUSIC LIMITED

12. I DREAMED A DREAM
(SCHÖNBERG/BOUBLIL/NATEL/KRETZMER)
WARNER/CHAPPELL NORTH AMERICA LIMITED

BACKING TRACKS ONLY

13. FÜR ELISE
14. LET IT BE
15. CLOCKS
16. THE ENTERTAINER
17. MINUET IN G
18. GREENSLEEVES
19. THE IRISH WASHERWOMAN
20. MUSIC BOX DANCER
21. THE CAN CAN
22. THEME FROM *SCHINDLER'S LIST*
23. JUPITER
24. I DREAMED A DREAM